Editing by Dally London
Front cover illustration by Dally London
All photographs by Phyllis Lane, Eric Cassée and Dally London
unless otherwise credited on page 241.
Hand illustrations by Dally London
Styled shot by @caseygoesclick, on page 195
Illustraion by A.C. Sparks, @a.c.sparks, on page 70
Calligraphy by Sidney Spurgeon @sidney.ink
Book design by Dally London

Published by Ex Artifex, LLC
dally.london.words@gmail.com

Free will says do what you want with my words and art.
Integrity says you shouldn't steal them and repurpose them as
your own. I say we're all dead anyway. So what can I control.

A world full of words allows imaginations to paint.

6.

56.

124.

176.

Forever

A

real

wolf

doesn't

chase

the

moon

to

prove

it

can

howl.

I DON'T CLAIM TO BE FLAWLESS

I JUST TRY TO BE FLAWED LESS.

Legends aren't remembered

for silver and gold,

legends are remembered,

for heart and soul.

Wild,

and alive,

chasing dreams,

in my mind.

DON'T LOSE SIGHT
OF THE ART WE ARE

The breath we breathe, the thoughts we believe, the beauty we see—it's all brilliant chemistry. We are the mathematical equation solved in a galaxy of complexity—a wine aged by the hands of time. We shine bright amongst a sea of stars. But we've lost sight of the art we are. Look in the mirror—for once try to see—all the variables connecting to bring about our destiny. We reflect the alchemy of life in this infinite night. We are brilliant design. We are the art of time.

WE'RE ALL IN A RELATIONSHIP WITH DEATH

SO MAKE EVERY
FUCKING BREATH,
COUNT.

Life winks at us every day,

for it knows the answers

to our questions,

but loves to watch us play.

Choose love. Choose to say what's in your heart and get the fuck out of your mind. We are a blink of time. There isn't a truthful tomorrow. The future is not a given. Breathe in this moment. Let life find your soul. Love now. Love it all.

Believe them when they say

'You are not a star.'

Prove them right.

Show them you are

a galaxy of light.

Seconds are the thieves

of life we forget steal on

death's behalf.

Every day I feel afraid—afraid of what the next moment will bring. If the afraid does not find you every day, you are living too comfortably. I do not mean be uncomfortable. But think—think today is not a given. I'm not sure when my eyes close for the night, I'll ever see the birth of tomorrow's day. I'm not sure my goodbye will mean forever or if it will simply mean the next time our eyes meet. We must find the forgotten happiness in each moment. The next second of life could bring about the fairytale or the curse. Even as you read these words, time is augmenting and altering who we are and what we are destined to become. We do not have the luxury of knowing the story time is writing for us.

There isn't a pause button on time. We have to accept we are in perpetual play. The clock is running and time—the only control we cannot control. All we can do is stare at it and watch as bystanders while it laughs with each tick. There are no takebacks. The last moments you've spent reading these words are lost forever. You cannot touch the past. You cannot undo the done. I only hope our souls carry on as life closes up shop. Maybe that's it. Maybe our dreams paint vivid manifestations of another life's time. Maybe they are gentle previews of what our next life will be. And maybe heaven is just a place hiding from time, where we all meet together as friends and say, *'Wasn't that a beautiful ride?'*

I chase my demons

to let them know

I run with them.

Speak from the depths of your soul—

let the world know what it feels like,

to live inside your bones.

Death never takes a day off,

so do not take days off life.

Only

cheap

fools

buy

their

own

hype.

A WARRIOR'S HEART

BEATS DEMONS

FROM THE SOUL.

HOW CRAZY IS LIFE'S DESIGN?

My words and your eyes,

were meant to meet,

at this specific time.

When snow falls on quiet nights,

listen to the snowflakes talk,

about their flight. And there in

the silence, if you listen clear,

you'll hear what angels sound

like, before they appear.

No one is above anyone,

we all taste the same sky,

we all feel the same sun.

I'll fight the rest of

these days awake,

for I've lived

far too long,

asleep.

Don't let your fire die,
risk it all,
with flames.

Life is a parallel dance of infinite infinities—music strummed by the fingertips of a smiling universe. Our ego tells us, '*we are it*'—that we are the pinnacle of intelligent design. But no—we thunder flesh and bone through infinite homes. We share brilliance with infinities of ourselves.

WE ARE STARS OF STARS.

This life is dying off so fast,

these words you read,

already live in the past.

TOMORROW HASN'T
BEEN BUILT YET.

Is tomorrow waiting for us to arrive? Or, is it being built when the choices of today arise? Do we paint time or is time painting us? Every second, we consume the future. Every next word you read lives in the future for your eyes to find, and now, lives in the past. Does existence exist before we experience it? Maybe time is just a collection of matter building the painting we project onto the construct of our physical life. Time is constantly at work to make the light show go. But what if the stars decide to stop shining? What if the sun doesn't come out to play or forgets to stay far, far away? Our tomorrow hasn't been built yet. Tomorrow isn't a constant though we assume it so. Tomorrow could be gone before it begins. So love right now. Treat the next word I write like it's the end.

We congregate around routines
because it feels safe. Fuck it.
Do something foreign. Make the
universe wonder about you for
a change.

I FLIRT WITH DEATH

TO REMIND MYSELF I'M ALIVE.

The once was may never be,

break up with the past,

let your heart start to dream.

THOSE WHO UNDERSTAND

THE SPACES BETWEEN SENTENCES

ARE THE ONES WHO ACTUALLY SEE.

Give pieces of yourself

to

those

who

complete

you.

real
magic
doesn't
disappear

THERE ARE NO PARADES FOR OUTLAW WAYS.

We bury ourselves in debt that starves our freedoms. We invert the application of life's design. We were not born into servitude. Inevitably we become the sheep forced to need the herder. Jobs eventually define us rather than us defining them. Life becomes a series of controls stealing its own intent from our grip. We're forced to follow the vision and belief of someone else's greed. We've become conditioned to accept the system. Freedom is an illusion. None of us are absolutely free. The idea of freedom can only come from open eyes, awake enough to see the controls by becoming outlaw thieves, learning how to steal back the system's ability to control. 'Things' should never be our definition. We should never empower 'things' to rob our freedoms. Date the stars instead of marrying houses and cars. Real freedom is in the heart and mind. Never be controlled by anything but time.

Everyone wears the mask of life. We occupy our minds with distractions from the inevitable curtain call of life's play. We bombard ourselves with tasks and stress hoping to suppress the weight of dying days resting on our shoulders. Allow your eyes to focus on the fact that every social media account you see is gone eventually. Every face you meet is dying. Every function we perform is a step towards a beautiful death. Time is but a wink on the smiling face of eternity. We are simply ghosts living in our skeleton's home, walking towards our graves alone.

IT'S SUCH A BEAUTIFUL

DEATH WE ALL POSSESS.

Let's watch the sunrays
paint clouds of a dying sunset,
while we wait for the sky
to grow twilight dandelions,
in the dark garden
of infinite dreams.

CHALLENGE IT ALL
LIFE WASN'T DESIGNED
TO WATCH US FALL.

Undone

AND WITH RUBBLE

FROM OUR CASTLE,

I BUILT A FORT

AROUND MY HEART.

I FEEL THE DEMONS
CRAWLING UP MY SPINE
A PRELUDE TO THE
CLOAK THEY'VE PREPARED TO
SUFFOCATE MY MIND

I let love *die*,

to see if it,

was still *alive*.

Heavy darkness drips the wild's breath into my eyes. The silent echoes, tremble my bones. I'm side-by-side with the alone. Walking the moon of the unknown forest— holding the cold compass of a frightened soul. My prayers journey for the sun to save me. The battle with blackness must win. I ready my sword, but cannot shake the monsters shaking me. Kill, or be killed. The bloom must grow thorns. I've become the alone.

Some

stars

are

meant

to

shine

alone.

Running away from the pain,

gives your demons stamina,

to remain.

FORGOTTEN FLOWERS

STILL BLOOM WILD.

A suicide of tears drips from my eyes,

while my heart suffocates to beat,

breathing out goodbye.

These razor blades salivate to wet their lips with the black blood dancing through me. They've grown eager to carve roads to my final heart beat. My wine is cursed with your elegant lies screaming to be released from its prison of hardened veins. My halo blackens with feelings of your poison. The universe flashes glimpses of our history while the stars fight with desire to litter black paint on the sink of this broken home. I whisky up my deadened soul—rinse thoughts of death from my mind. I feel your lies slither back into the dark beats of my heart. There's no sense in this theatre. I'm dead already.

Maybe you're the mistake I needed
to stop making them.

UNSPOKEN FEELINGS
WRITE NOVELS FOR
LONELY GRAVES.

L

O

V

E

FORGOTTEN LIPS MISS THE LOVE FROM A KISS.

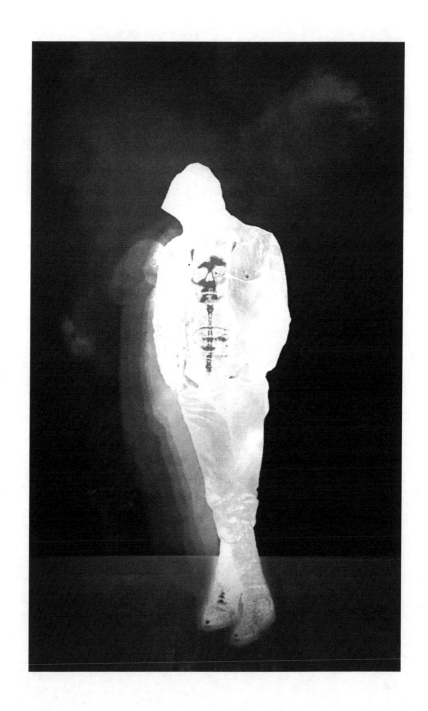

The alone

isn't alone at all

you see,

my demons

and monsters,

are always

beside me.

I

left

you

in

my

veins

too

long.

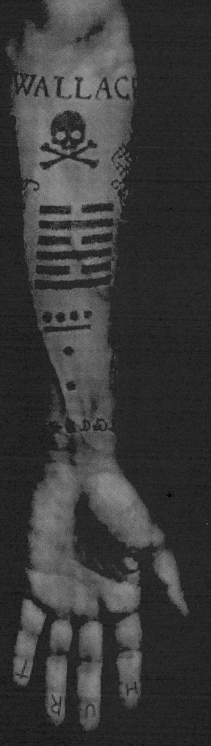

We had the universe,
but ignored the stars.

THESE NIGHTS ARE SO LONELY

I'VE BECOME FLUENT IN SILENCE.

Be gentle love,

my bones may be made of metal,

but I've a heart made of glass.

Sing life's song as we
slow dance with death.

My heart bled itself red to gray,

beating cold,

and alone,

as love died in its cage.

GARDENS OF HEARTACHE

GROW TO HELL.

Authenticity is the sexiest form of a soul. Unfortunately, it's sad how easily a blackened heart can alter its definition simply by projecting what they want the world to believe. Be cautious of the ones who tell you how great they are. Keep it fifty-fifty until you can judge the show behind the curtain. The quality of a person should never be defined by the number of followers next to a social media handle.

I THOUGHT I'D
FOUND MAGIC,
BUT YOU WERE
ONLY FULL OF
TRICKS.

At night I keep whisky,

resting by my side,

in case I need a taste of heaven,

right before I die.

Some days,

I wish we never met,

so I'd know

what

my

heart

feels

like,

not to have you to forget.

Whisky rainbows
follow trails to
broken heart's gold.

I wear heart scars like badges of
honour—witnesses to battles in love's
war—bled for the belief in a unified
heart beating love for one another.
Not every soul is worth the fight.
Never again shall I give my heart
away to slick palms, eager to want to
hold, but careless when they handle.

It's getting harder

and harder to know,

who's made of real

and who's made of

show.

Love's hurt me so often,

my butterflies grew fangs.

Some days I want to be in love.

Some days I rebel against the above.

Some days I would rather be alone.

Some days I curse my silent home.

Some days I can't live without a drink.

Some days I need to be sober to think.

Some days I want to be here.

Some days I feel death is near.

I've already dug my grave
by burying my soul in you.

dally london

Hearts heal slower than minds,

forget the pain one moment,

the heart beats to remind.

I see love all around me,

unfortunately it is me,

love forgets to see.

I DRINK WITH DEMONS

TO DREAM OF ANGELS.

Hearts deprived of
light learn to love
in the dark.

When you speak the alone,

you converse in a language,

only shadows know.

SOMETIMES ANGELS
NEED TO PAINT THEIR
WINGS WITH THE STARS.

You picked a flower

and never gave it sun,

then wondered why

the petals fell off,

one

by

one.

I no longer care about the ache,

my heart has been broken

so many times,

it's waiting on the break.

I've reflected so much on the past,

I could be a fucking antique mirror.

The
fairytale
is a
theoretical
hell.

I've prayed for love so much,

the gods told me to take a break,

maybe try my luck with lust.

I torched the lyrics of our song,

to hear what love sounds like,

when it goes up in flames.

We looked better in prose.

Happy masks
are worn by
Shattered Souls

— dally

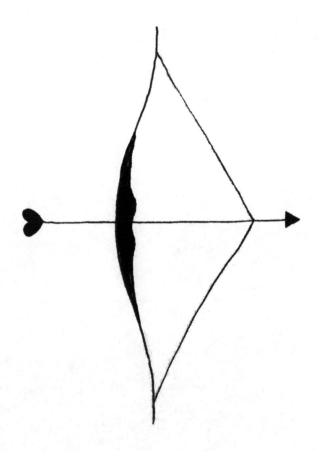

Maybe I should steal Cupid's arrow and shoot myself.

EVEN BONES MADE
OF THUNDER DREAM
OF RAINBOWS WHEN
THEY WONDER.

Let the tears fall.

Salt the seas of your ocean.

Find strength in the waves,

so when the storms come,

you can howl back.

Crave

Head over heels

is what they say,

I'm heart over mind,

fucked up that way.

I check the boxes love should fill, but it's one of life's equations, I've yet to fulfill. I hear my eyes are a bit too clear. I'm too intimidating with a beard. I'm too tall. I'm too nice. I think too much, as if that's some kind of vice. Does the universe curse me because I wear my heart on my sleeve? Well, truth be told, I wear my heart all over me. My love is able to be touched, but I never feel like it's enough. So I find safety behind these typewriter keys, but even cries for love echo back eventually. They reverberate my bones in a laughter that's grim, although maybe that's just the stars chuckling to love my light from within. But, I just can't seem to piece it all together. I tell myself every night, *'forget today, tomorrow will be better.'*

Kiss

me

like

you

want

to

taste

my

soul.

I WILL FIGHT THROUGH HELL

TO FIND YOUR HEAVEN.

WHEN I WALK MY LIPS UP YOUR THIGHS, I FEEL THE TAIL OF THE DEVIL

WHIPPING
THROUGH
MY MIND.

LET ME UNDRESS YOUR MIND.

We fight to see each other,

fight to make our days better,

fight through our hell together.

I LOVE HOW MUCH WE FIGHT.

'Until death do us part,'

the mind winked at the heart.

LET'S BE EACH OTHER'S SOLDIER

IN THIS BATTLE OF BROKEN HEARTS.

Dance

your

kisses

up

my

spine,

turn

me

into

wine.

Walk through life's haze—be the ember

setting your path ablaze. Let the fire of

your soul take control and feel the stars

take hold. Don't follow people, follow

freedom—change your own seasons.

Time whispers the end is ticking near.

Be the pioneer of your own years.

LIONS OF THE DARK

ROAR AT THE STARS

WITH THEIR HEARTS.

Trace my lips
with your tongue,
steal all the breath,
from my lungs.

Lust for one's mind

makes love think,

every time.

Talk to me in storms,
when you need to rage the rain.

I'll hold up your heaven,

while hell burns my back,

to protect you from the flames,

and keep your peace intact.

And when we touch the

fingertips of darkness,

I will meet you at the stars.

My heart isn't an

instrument of love—

it's a fucking

symphony.

SHARP DARTS ALWAYS HIT THEIR MARK

Let's breathe still amongst the chaos.

Press me up against the wall,

give my heart one more reason

to fall.

I'll

touch

the

edge,

to

taste

the

air

forever

breathes.

And we kiss,
like anarchists,
raging chaos
on desire's lips.

Colour

your

lips

with

my

skin.

When did it become such a sin,

to love the beauty on the outside,

and the beauty within?

My veins play as a violin,

when your symphony of love,

dances on my skin.

Let's love with peace and blood,

raging wars of romance

through thick and thin,

to keep the flame of our together,

lit forever within.

Hunt me like your

love soaked prey,

feast upon my naked heart,

while

you

lick

my

skin

with

flames.

I want a rebel,
a partner in crime,
who tries to steal my heart,
all the time.

Let's get whisky wild,

and pour our naked hearts,

into a sea of drunken love.

I want to
taste the
wild in
you

Sometimes,
you must run into the sunset,
to find your sunrise.

SEX WITH THE MIND
IS LIKE KISSES
MADE OF WINE.

I DON'T MIND A LITTLE BITE IF THE MOOD IS RIGHT

I'm drawn to the flames of your fire.

Tie

me

up

with

your

tongue,

tease

my

mind.

Fuck letting life pass by,

speak from a loving heart,

never let feelings die.

LET'S MAKE MAGICAL MAYHEM

Between us,
the unknown path,
we're both meant to walk.

Sometimes it's as if we love in reverse. At first, madly in love, then grow mad with our love. We eventually ignore the sun and forget the warmth we felt on day one. We take for granted what it's like to miss a morning kiss. We bury feelings in shadows and wonder why the butterflies never flit. We must fight falling asleep in love. We must make tomorrow today's run-on sentence. Never love enough. Love until the end of days. Then love some more. Be stubborn with forever ways.

We're the story
I want to tell.

LET'S
GET HIGH
TONIGHT,
AND DIVE
NAKED
INTO AN
OCEAN OF
STARS.

YOU TOUCH ME IN PLACES

NEVER TOUCHED BEFORE

THE PLACES IN MY HEART, NO ONE CARED TO EXPLORE.

I love switching between

your top and bottom lip,

to change the conversation,

of our kiss.

Deep

stars

reach

lost

hearts.

I awake to meet the morning,

your toes peek from the sheets,

it's the little things I notice,

that makes this life complete.

I CAME TO YOU IN PIECES

AND YOU LOVED ME BACK TOGETHER.

Let's have a one night sit,

and hookup with our minds,

about why we all exist.

WE'RE SO FUCKING
BEAUTIFUL IN LOVE.

I wish life had rewinds,

so I could meet you,

over and over again,

the very first time.

I don't want to grow old together,

I want to grow forever together.

With you by my side,

I feel the stars have already reached me.

YOU TAUGHT

MY SHADOWS

TO LOVE THE

LIGHT.

Those dimples,

when she smiles?

I could live in.

Let's be our breakfast in bed.

My

heart

and

mind

are

in

a

civil

war

with

time.

I'll hook my heart

around the moon,

and wait to play

in the stars with you.

Do you play connect the dots

with the stars, too?

I wonder,

will they ever show the path,

that leads my love to you?

You love me without saying a word,

your eyes,

your smile,

is forever being heard.

MY KISSES DON'T WANT TO EXIST

WITHOUT YOUR LIPS.

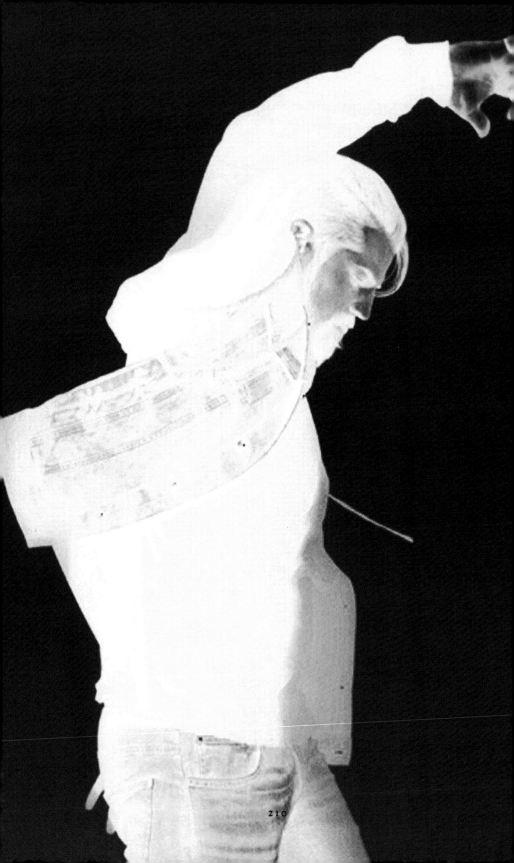

Let's skinny dip in the stars
and light the world
with our naked hearts.

I suffocate with butterflies

when I look into your eyes.

Let's hold our hearts
against each other,
and beat this world
together.

YOUR LOOKS MAY HAVE
CAUSED ME TO TRIP,
BUT YOUR MIND
CAUSED ME TO FALL.

I fell in love with your flaws,

the cute ones,

the bad ones—

I love them all.

there is
beauty in our
alchemy

It's hard to write about winter's cold,

when there's a summer love in you,

warming up my soul.

Our love in the morning feels different—
gravity navigating our bodies through
oceans of sheets to find each other for
the first time again. The feeling of your
skin. The smell of forever love—your
toes giving my calves a hug. Your breath
gliding across my chest, reminding
me morning cuddles are the best.

I LOVE WAKING NEXT TO YOU

I lose myself in your love,

which isn't losing,

at all.

HOW GORGEOUS YOU ARE,

IN A DRESS MADE OF STARS.

Your smell dances
cocaine footprints
through my soul.

Let's watch the sunset

kiss the snow,

as the fireplace

paints our toes

with

amber

glows.

I DIDN'T REALISE MY HEART COULD SPEAK

UNTIL YOU MADE IT TALK IN BEATS.

There's a space in your shoulder blade

where my cheekbone rests perfectly.

I call this my safe spot—a cozy nook

where my mind escapes to dream. Love's

puzzle is funny that way. Sometimes

the oddest pieces fit neatly together.

THE STARS PAINT PORTRAITS OF YOUR EYES.

Let's slow dance to the rhythm of forever.

We'll be together tomorrow,

even if I must leave you here,

today.

IF THERE IS A PARALLEL UNIVERSE

I WILL FIGHT THROUGH THE STARS TO FIND YOU.

FIN

GIANTS

I wish giants existed today, so we'd see the world through our animal's eyes, to make us rethink our ways.

They would speak a giant language, and we'd try to understand, we'd see them as a threat, but love them as a friend.

We'd do our best to keep these giants gentle, we'd charm them with our eyes, and show them cuteness in our dimples.

But we don't speak giant speak, you see, so we'd listen with great intentions, in hopes to obey in peace.

Although with some giants, our love would never be enough, no matter how cute we were, they would need to prove they're tough.

They'd hit our backs if we talked too much, and they'd yell at us in giant speak, for an item we shouldn't touch.

But we don't speak giant speak, so we'd try our best to understand and pray they only touch us, with gentle giant hands.

So think about this metaphor, when your animal does not understand, the things all us giants know, in a language they cannot comprehend.

Because they don't speak giant speak.

THANK YOU

I'm humbled on the daily by the hearts, the likes,
the notes I've received. Thank you for being a part
of my art and words, and giving this book a look.

SPECIAL THANKS

Mother, Brother, Chewy, Kristina, Kyle,

A.C. Sparks, Phyllis, Eric, Carrie, Abraham, Angie

PHOTOGRAPHY

Phyllis Lane, Eric Cassée, Dally London, Kristina

INSTAGRAM

@dallylondon

Our canvas is right now. We'll never get right now back. This exact moment will never be replicated. We're painting life's picture with every breath we breathe—every step we walk. Our eyes are constantly recording a movie we can never replay. Do not focus on the brush strokes of yesterday. Focus on the canvas of today. We're all artists in life's design. Let's paint a beautiful portrait for the stars and skies.

Much love

Made in the USA
Columbia, SC
20 August 2019